and
The Prophet
said…

and

The Prophet

said...

KAHLIL GIBRAN's
Classic Text *with*
Newly Discovered Writings

edited by
DALTON HILU EINHORN
WITH A FOREWORD BY DANIEL LADINSKY

HAMPTON ROADS

Cover and interior design by Kathryn Sky-Peck
Cover art, Merchant from Isfahan © Institute of Oriental Studies,
St. Petersburg, Russia / Bridgeman Images
Text illustrations by Kahlil Gibran
Typeset in Centaur

Hampton Roads Publishing Company, Inc.
Charlottesville, VA 22906
Distributed by Red Wheel/Weiser, LLC
www.redwheelweiser.com

Sign up for our newsletter and special offers by going to
www.redwheelweiser.com/newsletter.

ISBN: 978-1-64297-016-6
Library of Congress Cataloging-in-Publication Data available upon request.
Printed in Canada
MAR

10 9 8 7 6 5 4 3 2 1

To Virginia, with mutual delight
in the magic along the way, DHE

Louis Round Wilson Library
University of North Carolina
October 15, 2019

The editor wishes to thank Carlos Slim Helú for his passionate contribution to preserving and sharing the works and legacy of Kahlil Gibran. Like Gibran, Mr. Slim Helú was born to Lebanese Maronite Christian parents. The editor also wishes to thank the estate of Mary Haskell.

Contents

Foreword

I DISCOVERED KAHLIL GIBRAN as a young, troubled heart, so emotionally crippled at the time, that I could barely speak. He was a savior to me. His book, *The Prophet*, a wondrous oasis I could take refuge in, a true elixir. Reading it was as if he were sitting with me, as alive as you are, his words just what I had been waiting for. Millions have been touched by Gibran's love, lifted into the sun for a moment by his truth. His words hold us alight for a blessed second and help us with our glorious transformation, *from cocoon to wing*. In this book, Gibran expands that vital oasis, offering us his precious hand, so real that you can feel its pulse.

The idea of God, or Divine Beauty (or "the beloved" as Gibran refers to it at times) has many spiritual image terms: Father, Mother, Buddha, Self, Cosmic Me, The Thousand Suns, Christ Consciousness, or even *Super Wild Cowgirl*. In some ways God might be likened (although over simplified) to a *Grandfather*, content just hanging out in some greenhouse where ALL is contained, gazing for days at maybe just one flower, or just *one petal on a universe*. Inherent in true enlightenment is the ability to be in awe of anything, *forever*. The Persian mystic Hafiz once referred to all form and phenomena as, "The ground of conscious Nothing, but where the *Rose* does ever bloom." The Rose, being a symbol for the Absolute, or from where . . . *Light* does appear.

But this personification of love and knowledge—this Grandfather—in some ways really cares nothing about this world, as He/She/It is the root of non-attachment. All *but God* is a miraculous illusion. But that *Granddad* is there, grooving in the garden, but few, so very few can get close to such an all-powerful, magnificently sovereign, luminous Being. Or rarely does It *plant* anything so real into a dream, or a waking mystical experience so that one can become a true messenger to the world. Though if one can "get close," therein lies the transference of real power—the power to effect others. That *benevolent effect* can manifest via some exceptional contribution to science, to politics, as with someone like Gandhi, or through *creativity*, via music or the written word. Through his work, Kahlil Gibran is a true messenger to the world.

All prayer, in a way, is a tugging on the Grandfather's apron, an asking for help. And perhaps meditation and yoga, and reading illumined poetry and scripture, are much-needed forms of self-help. Or what Ralph Waldo-Emerson referred to in *Self-Reliance*. Or if one can: sometimes imbibing the *Presence* . . . which I think can happen when in awe with sublime (and even the simplest) aspects in nature, and in the firmament, can so benefit one via the purest of organic ways: *making love with beauty.*

How many *stressed ants* are star-struck? That is, how many of us have become so overwhelmed that we can't stop what we are doing long enough to peer into *the kingdom of heaven within,* or above? Or let our knees buckle in ecstasy from the wonder of the most common of things—a rock, a leaf, or that *bird*—that can be a universe unto itself. Gibran is there to remind us, to *guide us,* to be in gratitude and awe of even the simplest aspects of nature, and in the firmament, to refine our tastes and manners, and thus make our eyes and sounds . . . *more kind to every face.*

Gibran, whose first language was Arabic, would have known the word *wali.* It has a range of meanings: custodian, protector, helper, friend of the Beloved, friend of All, or saint. A book can become a wali. When so much intelligence, care, compassion, and insight are poured onto the page, a book develops a soul, as Gibran's works have. And just like a best friend . . . give them access to you 24/7, so too does God give access to friends and real helpers. And there are perks like: they get to slip their hands in the Beloved's pockets whenever they want, into some *divine cookie jar* as it were . . . and then can impart that sweetness—nutrients—to the world.

Water is most pure, and most nourishing, the closer to the spring you can get. Words are like that too. The words of Kahlil Gibran draw from the primordial Source of everything, the springhead. Was Gibran One with everything the way Buddha and Jesus were? Probably not. But he was surely entrusted with their wisdom and tenderness. He was a *true artist* and a wali. I once heard, from my own teacher, that God trusts the artist more than he does the priests, preachers, mullahs, and rabbis, to deliver His/ Her goods to the longing world.

The words—*the music*—in these pages come from the *Living Eternal Heart*. They are the soul of the rivers, the mountains, and the fields. They are the song of the stars and the planets. They are truly *Silence* speaking. Imbibe them, dear reader, throughout your life. And dance. *Dance!*

—Daniel Ladinsky,
International bestselling poet-author

Introduction

IN ITS FIRST ONE HUNDRED YEARS of life, Kahlil Gibran's masterpiece, *The Prophet*, cast a spell over generations, lifting it to the altitude of the most-purchased book of the twentieth century.

What Kahlil called his "curious little book" about a visitor on an island charmed millions with its antique voice, prose-poem structure, and Eastern spirituality. Now, nearly a century after its publication, *The Prophet* still stands out as an inspirational and guiding book of wisdom with few, if any, equals.

The roots of the story about an "Island Man" likely grew from a seed planted during Kahlil's childhood in Bcharre, Lebanon. But what was harvested as *The Prophet* was first transplanted to, nurtured, and cultivated in Kahlil's adopted home, the island of Manhattan.

There, where the son of Lebanon lived until his passing until 1931, Kahlil and his inspiration and soulmate, Mary Elizabeth Haskell, co-created what became many of the chapters of the book. Some of passages of *The Prophet* had their origins in conversations between Mary and Kahlil as they interacted with and dissected the world around them during times spent in New York City, particularly during the time period of 1916–1920.

As Kahlil and Mary walked among the masses of Midtown scurrying to their jobs, they discussed the concepts of what became the parable, "On Work," certainly influenced by seeing people unhappy as they toiled—thus, projecting that to some, labor was a curse. In the noisy chaos of their favorite restaurant, Gonafarone's in Greenwich Village, they observed couples and discussed the giving and receiving of love and how married women confided in Kahlil about their dissatisfactions with their husbands. These discussions formed the principles of the chapter, "On Marriage." On a bus inching along Fifth Avenue, Mary and Kahlil discussed the trial of the century, and "On Crime and Punishment" was born. Other passages were hatched while sitting near Grant's Tomb or reflecting in the peace of Kahlil's studio on West Tenth Street. So great is the importance of Mary that she is the inspiration for Almitra in *The Prophet.*

Thus, it is fitting that in this centennial edition of *The Prophet,* a treasure from Mary Haskell's possessions is offered in companion: a collection of never-published prose poems, a partial prose poem, nearly one-hundred aphorisms, and three chapters from *The Earth Gods* that were not included in the final edition.

When Kahlil Gibran passed on April 10, 1931, his Greenwich Village studio was filled with works in process—paintings, letters, sketches, and a set of writings intended for a new, short collection of prose poems. Gibran had written many of these poems in his native Arabic and had recently translated several into English, his adopted tongue.

After Kahlil's death, the contents of his studio were willed to Mary Haskell, whose role in Kahlil's life was known solely by his sister Mariana. Mary met Kahlil in 1904 and the two had a unique and secret loving relationship that transcended any definition known in that era or today. They considered marriage briefly, but their relationship evolved into a flowing confluence of teacher and student, inspiration and admirer, and an unfailing soulmate devotion. Mary encouraged Kahlil to write in English, and it was under her tutelage that he began the process of developing what he referred to as his great work.

During the years of the greatest output from her partnership with Kahlil, Mary struggled with the responsibility of running her school and began to feel exhausted. She began to consider the approaches of J. Florance Minis, a successful southern businessman and family friend, who implored her to move to Savannah, Georgia, where she could live a life of luxury with him. Although emotionally attached to Kahlil, Mary eventually relented and joined Florance in Savannah. In 1926, Mary and Florance married, and she was forced to maintain her relationship with Kahlil only in discreet privacy. However, upon learning of Kahlil's death, Mary suspended the discretion and gave all she felt was needed to honor her soulmate and to preserve his legacy.

Mary managed nearly all of Kahlil's affairs after his death, arranging the return of his mortal remains to his

Mary Haskell by Kahlil Gibran, 1910

beloved Lebanon. She ensured, as the will specified, that his financial holdings were given to Mariana. Kahlil's possessions, by then valuable for their connection to *The Prophet*, belonged to Mary.

Furniture, personal belongings, and more than 400 original paintings from Gibran's studio were donated by Mary to the town of Bcharre. They form basis of The Gibran Museum located in the former Monastery of Mar Sarkis, which was built in the seventh century as a grotto for monks seeking shelter.

Mary kept some sketches and paintings at her home in Savannah, Georgia, as reminders of her treasured friend. In 1950, at the age of seventy-seven, Mary donated most of the artwork to the Telfair Museum in Savannah, which now houses the largest public collection of Gibran's visual art in the United States.

In 1960, four years before her death, Mary donated her papers to the University of North Carolina, Chapel Hill. There was historical interest in accepting the donation—the University knew that the Minis family history stretched into colonial Georgia, and among the more famous Haskell family members was the former colonel who was instructed by Robert E. Lee to surrender the Confederate cavalry at Appomattox Court House, bringing the fighting of the Civil War to an end.

When a librarian cataloging the collection stumbled upon thousands of pages of writings about, to, and from Kahlil Gibran, she was stunned. Here in the librarian's hands were thousands of pages of writings that told a complicated love story that had been kept secret for decades. And tucked into those files were unpublished writings that sat waiting for Kahlil to return to them and be developed into what was intended to be a new book.

My mother, Virginia Hilu, was hired by the estates of Kahlil and Mary to produce a book from these thousands of pages of material. In 1972, Alfred A. Knopf published *Beloved Prophet*, a selection of journal entries and letters that introduced Mary Haskell, chronicled Kahlil's growth from boyish artist to internationally known figure, and told of an improbable, hidden love story.

Additional books were intended to follow, but my mother died at the age of forty-seven from the cancer that was diagnosed as she edited the Gibran-Haskell materials. She never began work on a second book.

I was seven when she died and grew up in a fractured family unable to cope with her loss. Upon my fortieth birthday, I realized I knew little about her and I thought that I could achieve closure by learning about her twenty-three year career in the publishing industry and the story of her most successful book, *Beloved Prophet*. But first, I felt I had to read Kahlil's books and that none was more important than *The Prophet*.

I bought a hardcover copy of *The Prophet*, which arrived in the fall of 2011. Kahlil was a lover of storms but could not have found joy in what soon transpired, the devastating hurricane, Sandy. Without power for eleven days, I had nothing but time to read. Perhaps adding to the dramatic effect, I sat down one evening, lantern in hand, for my first experience reading the words of Kahlil Gibran.

The lamp swung and hit the corner the book, which fell open. I picked up *The Prophet* and read the passage on the open page:

> *"Brief were my days among you, and briefer still the words I have spoken.*
>
> *But should my voice fade in your ears, and my love vanish in your memory, then I will come again,*
>
> *And with a richer heart and lips more yielding to the spirit will I speak."*

My mother's voice came to me again. My reaction to *The Prophet* was likely similar to those of many who read Kahlil's works: I felt the words were written just for me. And from that moment I was inspired to finish the work Virginia Hilu started and to publish from the pages of Mary Haskell's collection, which I knew my mother had held with her own hands decades earlier.

⟶

The unpublished writings presented here are part of The Southern Historical Collection at the Louis Round Wilson Special Collections Library of the University of North Carolina houses Collection 02725: "Minis Family Papers, 1739–1948." Subseries 2.4, "Kahlil Gibran

Materials, 1904–1931 and undated." Folders 276–277 are labeled "writings."

The writings published in this book are presented in the order in which they were found during my research at UNC in 2017 and 2018, which likely varies from their in-situ condition in 1960. No information currently available accurately catalogues the original state of the archives.

Sixteen poems that seem to be complete are offered here, two of which are untitled. Based on notes found in the files, it appears that at the time of his death, Gibran was in the process of translating poems he had written previously in Arabic. One poem appears to have been written in 1908; another is identified as the last poem translated by Gibran before his death.

One poem is clearly incomplete. The fate of the remainder of that poem is unknown. A lost page? A translation interrupted by death?

Fragments of writings were found, as if they were from Gibran's notebook. Several fragments were published as is, or in similar form, in other published writings of Gibran. Ninety-nine fragments are contained in this book—none of which were identified as being published previously. Perhaps those would have become prose poems had he lived.

Three draft sections of *The Earth Gods* are presented that contain writing that was not later used. However, these sections struck me as meaningful, so I have included them here.

The writings of Kahlil Gibran and Mary Haskell that are found in Subseries 2.4 ("Kahlil Gibran Materials, 1904–1931 and undated") are protected by copyright and may be reproduced only with explicit permissions in writing from their owners. Permissions were received from both the Gibran and Haskell estates to proceed with this publication.

Like my own odyssey, it seemed fitting to open this collection with *The Prophet*, Gibran's seminal work, originally published in 1923, and which saw its copyright expire in 2019. All unpublished work that I found in my research follows it. Through these pages, let us rejoice again in Kahlil's original work and let him speak to us anew.

Part One

The Prophet

The twelve illustrations in The Prophet
*are reproduced from original drawings
by the author.*

Almustafa, the chosen and the beloved, who was a dawn unto his own day, had waited twelve years in the city of Orphalese for his ship that was to return and bear him back to the isle of his birth.

And in the twelfth year, on the seventh day of Ielool, the month of reaping, he climbed the hill without the city walls and looked seaward; and he beheld his ship coming with the mist.

Then the gates of his heart were flung open, and his joy flew far over the sea. And he closed his eyes and prayed in the silences of his soul.

But as he descended the hill, a sadness came upon him, and he thought in his heart:

How shall I go in peace and without sorrow? Nay, not without a wound in the spirit shall I leave this city.

Long were the days of pain I have spent within its walls, and long were the nights of aloneness; and who can depart from his pain and his aloneness without regret?

Too many fragments of the spirit have I scattered in these streets, and too many are the children of my longing that walk naked among these hills, and I cannot withdraw from them without a burden and an ache.

It is not a garment I cast off this day, but a skin that I tear with my own hands.

Nor is it a thought I leave behind me, but a heart made sweet with hunger and with thirst.

Yet I cannot tarry longer.

The sea that calls all things unto her calls me, and I must embark.

For to stay, though the hours burn in the night, is to freeze and crystallize and be bound in a mould.

Fain would I take with me all that is here. But how shall I?

A voice cannot carry the tongue and the lips that gave it wings. Alone must it seek the ether.

And alone and without his nest shall the eagle fly across the sun.

Now when he reached the foot of the hill, he turned again towards the sea, and he saw his ship approaching the harbour, and upon her prow the mariners, the men of his own land.

And his soul cried out to them, and he said:

Sons of my ancient mother, you riders of the tides,

How often have you sailed in my dreams. And now you come in my awakening, which is my deeper dream.

Ready am I to go, and my eagerness with sails full set awaits the wind.

Only another breath will I breathe in this still air, only another loving look cast backward,

And then I shall stand among you, a seafarer among seafarers. And you, vast sea, sleepless mother,

Who alone are peace and freedom to the river and the stream,

Only another winding will this stream make, only another murmur in this glade,

And then shall I come to you, a boundless drop to a boundless ocean.

And as he walked he saw from afar men and women leaving their fields and their vineyards and hastening towards the city gates.

And he heard their voices calling his name, and shouting from field to field telling one another of the coming of his ship.

And he said to himself:

Shall the day of parting be the day of gathering?

And shall it be said that my eve was in truth my dawn?

And what shall I give unto him who has left his plough in midfurrow, or to him who has stopped the wheel of his winepress?

Shall my heart become a tree heavy-laden with fruit that I may gather and give unto them?

And shall my desires flow like a fountain that I may fill their cups?

Am I a harp that the hand of the mighty may touch me, or a flute that his breath may pass through me?

A seeker of silences am I, and what treasure have I found in silences that I may dispense with confidence?

If this is my day of harvest, in what fields have I sowed the seed, and in what unremembered seasons?

If this indeed be the the hour in which I lift up my lantern, it is not my flame that shall burn therein.

Empty and dark shall I raise my lantern,

And the guardian of the night shall fill it with oil and he shall light it also.

These things he said in words. But much in his heart remained unsaid. For he himself could not speak his deeper secret.

And when he entered into the city all the people came to meet him, and they were crying out to him as with one voice.

And the elders of the city stood forth and said:

Go not yet away from us.

A noontide have you been in our twilight, and your youth has given us dreams to dream.

No stranger are you among us, nor a guest, but our son and our dearly beloved.

Suffer not yet our eyes to hunger for your face.

And the priests and the priestesses said unto him:

Let not the waves of the sea separate us now, and the years you have spent in our midst become a memory.

You have walked among us a spirit, and your shadow has been a light upon our faces.

Much have we loved you. But speechless was our love, and with veils has it been veiled.

Yet now it cries aloud unto you, and would stand revealed before you.

And ever has it been that love knows not its own depth until the hour of separation.

And others came also and entreated him. But he answered them not. He only bent his head; and those who stood near saw his tears falling upon his breast.

And he and the people proceeded towards the great square before the temple.

And there came out of the sanctuary a woman whose name was Almitra. And she was a seeress.

And he looked upon her with exceeding tenderness, for it was she who had first sought and believed in him when he had been but a day in their city.

And she hailed him, saying:

Prophet of God, in quest of the uttermost, long have you searched the distances for your ship.

And now your ship has come, and you must needs go.

Deep is your longing for the land of your memories and the dwelling place of your greater desires; and our love would not bind you nor our needs hold you.

Yet this we ask ere you leave us, that you speak to us and give us of your truth.

And we will give it unto our children, and they unto their children, and it shall not perish.

In your aloneness you have watched with our days, and in your wakefulness you have listened to the weeping and the laughter of your sleep.

Now therefore disclose us to ourselves, and tell us all that has been shown you of that which is between birth and death.

And he answered,
People of Orphalese, of what can I speak save of that which is even now moving within your souls?

Then said Almitra, Speak to us of Love.

And he raised his head and looked upon the people, and there fell a stillness upon them. And with a great voice he said:

When love beckons to you, follow him,

Though his ways are hard and steep.

And when his wings enfold you yield to him,

Though the sword hidden among his pinions may wound you.

And when he speaks to you believe in him,

Though his voice may shatter your dreams as the north wind lays waste the garden.

For even as love crowns you so shall he crucify you. Even as he is for your growth so is he for your pruning.

Even as he ascends to your height and caresses your tenderest branches that quiver in the sun,

So shall he descend to your roots and shake them in their clinging to the earth.

Like sheaves of corn he gathers you unto himself.

He threshes you to make you naked.

He sifts you to free you from your husks.

He grinds you to whiteness.

He kneads you until you are pliant;

And then he assigns you to his sacred fire, that you may become sacred bread for God's sacred feast.

All these things shall love do unto you that you may know the secrets of your heart, and in that knowledge become a fragment of Life's heart.

But if in your fear you would seek only love's peace and love's pleasure,
Then it is better for you that you cover your nakedness and pass out of love's threshing-floor,
Into the seasonless world where you shall laugh, but not all of your laughter, and weep, but not all of your tears.

Love gives naught but itself and takes naught but from itself.
Love possesses not nor would it be possessed;
For love is sufficient unto love.

When you love you should not say, "God is in my heart," but rather, "I am in the heart of God."
And think not you can direct the course of love, for love, if it finds you worthy, directs your course.

Love has no other desire but to fulfil itself.
But if you love and must needs have desires, let these be your desires:
To melt and be like a running brook that sings its melody to the night. To know the pain of too much tenderness.

To be wounded by your own understanding of love;
And to bleed willingly and joyfully.

To wake at dawn with a winged heart and give thanks
for another day of loving;

To rest at the noon hour and meditate love's ecstacy;

To return home at eventide with gratitude;

And then to sleep with a prayer for the beloved in your
heart and a song of praise upon your lips.

hen Almitra spoke again and said, And what of Marriage master?

And he answered saying:

You were born together, and together you shall be forevermore.

You shall be together when the white wings of death scatter your days.

Ay, you shall be together even in the silent memory of God.

But let there be spaces in your togetherness,

And let the winds of the heavens dance between you.

Love one another, but make not a bond of love:

Let it rather be a moving sea between the shores of your souls.

Fill each other's cup but drink not from one cup.

Give one another of your bread but eat not from the same loaf.

Sing and dance together and be joyous, but let each one of you be alone,

Even as the strings of a lute are alone though they quiver with the same music.

Give your hearts, but not into each other's keeping.

For only the hand of Life can contain your hearts.

And stand together yet not too near together:

For the pillars of the temple stand apart,

And the oak tree and the cypress grow not in each other's shadow.

nd a woman who held a babe against her bosom said, Speak to us of Children.

And he said:

Your children are not your children.

They are the sons and daughters of Life's longing for itself.

They come through you but not from you,

And though they are with you yet they belong not to you.

You may give them your love but not your thoughts,

For they have their own thoughts.

You may house their bodies but not their souls,

For their souls dwell in the house of tomorrow, which you cannot visit, not even in your dreams.

You may strive to be like them, but seek not to make them like you.

For life goes not backward nor tarries with yesterday.

You are the bows from which your children as living arrows are sent forth.

The archer sees the mark upon the path of the infinite, and He bends you with His might that His arrows may go swift and far.

Let your bending in the Archer's hand be for gladness;

For even as He loves the arrow that flies, so He loves also the bow that is stable.

hen said a rich man, Speak to us of Giving.

And he answered:

You give but little when you give of your possessions.

It is when you give of yourself that you truly give.

For what are your possessions but things you keep and guard for fear you may need them tomorrow?

And tomorrow, what shall tomorrow bring to the overprudent dog burying bones in the trackless sand as he follows the pilgrims to the holy city?

And what is fear of need but need itself?

Is not dread of thirst when your well is full, the thirst that is unquenchable?

There are those who give little of the much which they have—and they give it for recognition and their hidden desire makes their gifts unwholesome.

And there are those who have little and give it all.

These are the believers in life and the bounty of life, and their coffer is never empty.

There are those who give with joy, and that joy is their reward.

And there are those who give with pain, and that pain is their baptism.

And there are those who give and know not pain in giving, nor do they seek joy, nor give with mindfulness of virtue;

They give as in yonder valley the myrtle breathes its fragrance into space.

Through the hands of such as these God speaks, and from behind their eyes He smiles upon the earth.

It is well to give when asked, but it is better to give unasked, through understanding;
And to the open-handed the search for one who shall receive is joy greater than giving.
And is there aught you would withhold?
All you have shall some day be given;
Therefore give now, that the season of giving may be yours and not your inheritors'.

You often say, "I would give, but only to the deserving."
The trees in your orchard say not so, nor the flocks in your pasture.
They give that they may live, for to withhold is to perish.
Surely he who is worthy to receive his days and his nights, is worthy of all else from you.
And he who has deserved to drink from the ocean of life deserves to fill his cup from your little stream.
And what desert greater shall there be, than that which lies in the courage and the confidence, nay the charity, of receiving?
And who are you that men should rend their bosom and unveil their pride, that you may see their worth naked and their pride unabashed?
See first that you yourself deserve to be a giver, and an instrument of giving.

For in truth it is life that gives unto life—while you, who deem yourself a giver, are but a witness.

And you receivers—and you are all receivers—assume no weight of gratitude, lest you lay a yoke upon yourself and upon him who gives.

Rather rise together with the giver on his gifts as on wings;

For to be overmindful of your debt, is ito doubt his generosity who has the freehearted earth for mother, and God for father.

hen an old man, a keeper of an inn, said, Speak to us of Eating and Drinking.

And he said:

Would that you could live on the fragrance of the earth, and like an air plant be sustained by the light.

But since you must kill to eat, and rob the newly born of its mother's milk to quench your thirst, let it then be an act of worship.

And let your board stand an altar on which the pure and the innocent of forest and plain are sacrificed for that which is purer and still more innocent in man.

When you kill a beast say to him in your heart,

"By the same power that slays you, I too am slain; and I too shall be consumed.

For the law that delivered you into my hand shall deliver me into a mightier hand.

Your blood and my blood is naught but the sap that feeds the tree of heaven.

And when you crush an apple with your teeth, say to it in your heart,

"Your seeds shall live in my body,

And the buds of your tomorrow shall blossom in my heart,

And your fragrance shall be my breath,

And together we shall rejoice through all the seasons."

And in the autumn, when you gather the grapes of your vineyards for the winepress, say in your heart,

"I too am a vineyard, and my fruit shall be gathered for the winepress,

And like new wine I shall be kept in eternal vessels."

And in winter, when you draw the wine, let there be in your heart a song for each cup;

And let there be in the song a remembrance for the autumn days, and for the vineyard, and for the winepress.

Then a ploughman said, Speak to us of Work.

And he answered, saying:

You work that you may keep pace with the earth and the soul of the earth.

For to be idle is to become a stranger unto the seasons, and to step out of life's procession, that marches in majesty and proud submission towards the infinite.

When you work you are a flute through whose heart the whispering of the hours turns to music.

Which of you would be a reed, dumb and silent, when all else sings together in unison?

Always you have been told that work is a curse and labour a misfortune.

But I say to you that when you work you fulfil a part of earth's furthest dream, assigned to you when that dream was born,

And in keeping yourself with labour you are in truth loving life,

And to love life through labour is to be intimate with life's inmost secret.

But if you in your pain call birth an affliction and the support of the flesh a curse written upon your brow, then I answer that naught but the sweat of your brow shall wash away that which is written.

You have been told also that life is darkness, and in your weariness you echo what was said by the weary.

And I say that life is indeed darkness save when there is urge,

And all urge is blind save when there is knowledge,

And all knowledge is vain save when there is work,

And all work is empty save when there is love;

And when you work with love you bind yourself to yourself, and to one another, and to God.

And what is it to work with love?

It is to weave the cloth with threads drawn from your heart, even as if your beloved were to wear that cloth.

It is to build a house with affection, even as if your beloved were to dwell in that house.

It is to sow seeds with tenderness and reap the harvest with joy, even as if your beloved were to eat the fruit.

It is to charge all things you fashion with a breath of your own spirit,

And to know that all the blessed dead are standing about you and watching.

Often have I heard you say, as if speaking in sleep, "He who works in marble, and finds the shape of his own soul in the stone, is nobler than he who ploughs the soil.

And he who seizes the rainbow to lay it on a cloth in the likeness of man, is more than he who makes the sandals for our feet."

But I say, not in sleep but in the overwakefulness of noontide, that the wind speaks not more sweetly to the giant oaks than to the least of all the blades of grass;

And he alone is great who turns the voice of the wind into a song made sweeter by his own loving.

Work is love made visible.

And if you cannot work with love but only with distaste, it is better that you should leave your work and sit at the gate of the temple and take alms of those who work with joy.

For if you bake bread with indifference, you bake a bitter bread that feeds but half man's hunger.

And if you grudge the crushing of the grapes, your grudge distils a poison in the wine. And if you sing though as angels, and love not the singing, you muffle man's ears to the voices of the day and the voices of the night.

hen a woman said, Speak to us of Joy and Sorrow. And he answered:

Your joy is your sorrow unmasked.

And the selfsame well from which your laughter rises was oftentimes filled with your tears.

And how else can it be?

The deeper that sorrow carves into your being, the more joy you can contain.

Is not the cup that holds your wine the very cup that was burned in the potter's oven?

And is not the lute that soothes your spirit, the very wood that was hollowed with knives?

When you are joyous, look deep into your heart and you shall find it is only that which has given you sorrow that is giving you joy.

When you are sorrowful look again in your heart, and you shall see that in truth you are weeping for that which has been your delight.

Some of you say, "Joy is greater than sorrow," and others say, "Nay, sorrow is the greater."

But I say unto you, they are inseparable.

Together they come, and when one sits alone with you at your board, remember that the other is asleep upon your bed.

Verily you are suspended like scales between your sorrow and your joy.

Only when you are empty are you at standstill and balanced.

When the treasure-keeper lifts you to weigh his gold and his silver, needs must your joy or your sorrow rise or fall.

hen a mason came forth and said, Speak to us of Houses.

And he answered and said:

Build of your imaginings a bower in the wilderness ere you build a house within the city walls.

For even as you have home-comings in your twilight, so has the wanderer in you, the ever distant and alone.

Your house is your larger body.

It grows in the sun and sleeps in the stillness of the night; and it is not dreamless. Does not your house dream? and dreaming, leave the city for grove or hill-top?

Would that I could gather your houses into my hand, and like a sower scatter them in forest and meadow.

Would the valleys were your streets, and the green paths your alleys, that you might seek one another through vineyards, and come with the fragrance of the earth in your garments.

But these things are not yet to be.

In their fear your forefathers gathered you too near together. And that fear shall endure a little longer. A little longer shall your city walls separate your hearths from your fields.

And tell me, people of Orphalese, what have you in these houses? And what is it you guard with fastened doors?

Have you peace, the quiet urge that reveals your power?

Have you remembrances, the glimmering arches that span the summits of the mind?

Have you beauty, that leads the heart from things fashioned of wood and stone to the holy mountain?

Tell me, have you these in your houses?

Or have you only comfort, and the lust for comfort, that stealthy thing that enters the house a guest, and then becomes a host, and then a master?

Ay, and it becomes a tamer, and with hook and scourge makes puppets of your larger desires.

Though its hands are silken, its heart is of iron.

It lulls you to sleep only to stand by your bed and jeer at the dignity of the flesh.

It makes mock of your sound senses, and lays them in thistledown like fragile vessels.

Verily the lust for comfort murders the passion of the soul, and then walks grinning in the funeral.

But you, children of space, you restless in rest, you shall not be trapped nor tamed.

Your house shall be not an anchor but a mast.

It shall not be a glistening film that covers a wound, but an eyelid that guards the eye.

You shall not fold your wings that you may pass through doors, nor bend your heads that they strike not against a ceiling, nor fear to breathe lest walls should crack and fall down.

You shall not dwell in tombs made by the dead for the living.

And though of magnificence and splendour, your house shall not hold your secret nor shelter your longing.

For that which is boundless in you abides in the mansion of the sky, whose door is the morning mist, and whose windows are the songs and the silences of night.

nd the weaver said, Speak to us of Clothes.

And he answered:

Your clothes conceal much of your beauty, yet they hide not the unbeautiful.

And though you seek in garments the freedom of privacy you may find in them a harness and a chain.

Would that you could meet the sun and the wind with more of your skin and less of your raiment,

For the breath of life is in the sunlight and the hand of life is in the wind.

Some of you say, "It is the north wind who has woven the clothes we wear."

And I say, Ay, it was the north wind,

But shame was his loom, and the softening of the sinews was his thread.

And when his work was done he laughed in the forest.

Forget not that modesty is for a shield against the eye of the unclean.

And when the unclean shall be no more, what were modesty but a fetter and a fouling of the mind?

And forget not that the earth delights to feel your bare feet and the winds long to play with your hair.

nd a merchant said, Speak to us of Buying and Selling.

And he answered and said:

To you the earth yields her fruit, and you shall not want if you but know how to fill your hands.

It is in exchanging the gifts of the earth that you shall find abundance and be satisfied.

Yet unless the exchange be in love and kindly justice, it will but lead some to greed and others to hunger.

When in the market place you toilers of the sea and fields and vineyards meet the weavers and the potters and the gatherers of spices,—

Invoke then the master spirit of the earth, to come into your midst and sanctify the scales and the reckoning that weighs value against value.

And suffer not the barren-handed to take part in your transactions, who would sell their words for your labour.

To such men you should say,

"Come with us to the field, or go with our brothers to the sea and cast your net;

For the land and the sea shall be bountiful to you even as to us."

And if there come the singers and the dancers and the flute players,—buy of their gifts also.

For they too are gatherers of fruit and frankincense, and that which they bring, though fashioned of dreams, is raiment and food for your soul.

And before you leave the market place, see that no one has gone his way with empty hands.

For the master spirit of the earth shall not sleep peacefully upon the wind till the needs of the least of you are satisfied.

Then one of the judges of the city stood forth and said, Speak to us of Crime and Punishment.

And he answered, saying:

It is when your spirit goes wandering upon the wind,

That you, alone and unguarded, commit a wrong unto others and therefore unto yourself.

And for that wrong committed must you knock and wait a while unheeded at the gate of the blessed.

Like the ocean is your god-self;

It remains for ever undefiled.

And like the ether it lifts but the winged.

Even like the sun is your god-self;

It knows not the ways of the mole nor seeks it the holes of the serpent.

But your god-self dwells not alone in your being.

Much in you is still man, and much in you is not yet man,

But a shapeless pigmy that walks asleep in the mist searching for its own awakening.

And of the man in you would I now speak.

For it is he and not your god-self nor the pigmy in the mist, that knows crime and the punishment of crime.

Oftentimes have I heard you speak of one who commits a wrong as though he were not one of you, but a stranger unto you and an intruder upon your world.

But I say that even as the holy and the righteous cannot rise beyond the highest which is in each one of you,

So the wicked and the weak cannot fall lower than the lowest which is in you also.

And as a single leaf turns not yellow but with the silent knowledge of the whole tree,

So the wrong-doer cannot do wrong without the hidden will of you all.

Like a procession you walk together towards your god-self.

You are the way and the wayfarers.

And when one of you falls down he falls for those behind him, a caution against the stumbling stone.

Ay, and he falls for those ahead of him, who though faster and surer of foot, yet removed not the stumbling stone.

And this also, though the word lie heavy upon your hearts:

The murdered is not unaccountable for his own murder,

And the robbed is not blameless in being robbed.

The righteous is not innocent of the deeds of the wicked,

And the white-handed is not clean in the doings of the felon.

Yea, the guilty is oftentimes the victim of the injured,

And still more often the condemned is the burden bearer for the guiltless and unblamed.

You cannot separate the just from the unjust and the good from the wicked;

For they stand together before the face of the sun even as the black thread and the white are woven together.

And when the black thread breaks, the weaver shall look into the whole cloth, and he shall examine the loom also.

If any of you would bring to judgment the unfaithful wife,

Let him also weigh the heart of her husband in scales, and measure his soul with measurements.

And let him who would lash the offender look unto the spirit of the offended.

And if any of you would punish in the name of righteousness and lay the ax unto the evil tree, let him see to its roots;

And verily he will find the roots of the good and the bad, the fruitful and the fruitless, all entwined together in the silent heart of the earth.

And you judges who would be just,

What judgment pronounce you upon him who though honest in the flesh yet is a thief in spirit?

What penalty lay you upon him who slays in the flesh yet is himself slain in the spirit?

And how prosecute you him who in action is a deceiver and an oppressor,

Yet who also is aggrieved and outraged?

And how shall you punish those whose remorse is already greater than their misdeeds?

Is not remorse the justice which is administered by that very law which you would fain serve?

Yet you cannot lay remorse upon the innocent nor lift it from the heart of the guilty.

Unbidden shall it call in the night, that men may wake and gaze upon themselves.

And you who would understand justice, how shall you unless you look upon all deeds in the fullness of light?

Only then shall you know that the erect and the fallen are but one man standing in twilight between the night of his pigmy-self and the day of his god-self,

And that the corner-stone of the temple is not higher than the lowest stone in its foundation.

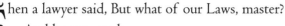

hen a lawyer said, But what of our Laws, master?

And he answered:

You delight in laying down laws,

Yet you delight more in breaking them.

Like children playing by the ocean who build sand-towers with constancy and then destroy them with laughter.

But while you build your sand-towers the ocean brings more sand to the shore,

And when you destroy them the ocean laughs with you.

Verily the ocean laughs always with the innocent.

But what of those to whom life is not an ocean, and man-made laws are not sand-towers,

But to whom life is a rock, and the law a chisel with which they would carve it in their own likeness?

What of the cripple who hates dancers?

What of the ox who loves his yoke and deems the elk and deer of the forest stray and vagrant things?

What of the old serpent who cannot shed his skin, and calls all others naked and shameless?

And of him who comes early to the wedding-feast, and when over-fed and tired goes his way saying that all feasts are violation and all feasters lawbreakers?

What shall I say of these save that they too stand in the sunlight, but with their backs to the sun?

They see only their shadows, and their shadows are their laws.

And what is the sun to them but a caster of shadows?

And what is it to acknowledge the laws but to stoop down and trace their shadows upon the earth?

But you who walk facing the sun, what images drawn on the earth can hold you?

You who travel with the wind, what weather-vane shall direct your course?

What man's law shall bind you if you break your yoke but upon no man's prison door?

What laws shall you fear if you dance but stumble against no man's iron chains?

And who is he that shall bring you to judgment if you tear off your garment yet leave it in no man's path?

People of Orphalese, you can muffle the drum, and you can loosen the strings of the lyre, but who shall command the skylark not to sing?

nd an orator said, Speak to us of Freedom.

And he answered:

At the city gate and by your fireside I have seen you prostrate yourself and worship your own freedom,

Even as slaves humble themselves before a tyrant and praise him though he slays them.

Ay, in the grove of the temple and in the shadow of the citadel I have seen the freest among you wear their freedom as a yoke and a handcuff.

And my heart bled within me; for you can only be free when even the desire of seeking freedom becomes a harness to you, and when you cease to speak of freedom as a goal and a fulfilment.

You shall be free indeed when your days are not without a care nor your nights without a want and a grief,

But rather when these things girdle your life and yet you rise above them naked and unbound.

And how shall you rise beyond your days and nights unless you break the chains which you at the dawn of your understanding have fastened around your noon hour?

In truth that which you call freedom is the strongest of these chains, though its links glitter in the sun and dazzle your eyes.

And what is it but fragments of your own self you would discard that you may become free?

If it is an unjust law you would abolish, that law was written with your own hand upon your own forehead.

You cannot erase it by burning your law books nor by washing the foreheads of your judges, though you pour the sea upon them.

And if it is a despot you would dethrone, see first that his throne erected within you is destroyed.

For how can a tyrant rule the free and the proud, but for a tyranny in their own freedom and a shame in their own pride?

And if it is a care you would cast off, that cart has been chosen by you rather than imposed upon you.

And if it is a fear you would dispel, the seat of that fear is in your heart and not in the hand of the feared.

Verily all things move within your being in constant half embrace, the desired and the dreaded, the repugnant and the cherished, the pursued and that which you would escape.

These things move within you as lights and shadows in pairs that cling.

And when the shadow fades and is no more, the light that lingers becomes a shadow to another light.

And thus your freedom when it loses its fetters becomes itself the fetter of a greater freedom.

nd the priestess spoke again and said: Speak to us of Reason and Passion.

And he answered, saying:

Your soul is oftentimes a battlefield, upon which your reason and your judgment wage war against your passion and your appetite.

Would that I could be the peacemaker in your soul, that I might turn the discord and the rivalry of your elements into oneness and melody.

But how shall I, unless you yourselves be also the peacemakers, nay, the lovers of all your elements?

Your reason and your passion are the rudder and the sails of your seafaring soul.

If either your sails or your rudder be broken, you can but toss and drift, or else be held at a standstill in mid-seas.

For reason, ruling alone, is a force confining; and passion, unattended, is a flame that burns to its own destruction.

Therefore let your soul exalt your reason to the height of passion, that it may sing;

And let it direct your passion with reason, that your passion may live through its own daily resurrection, and like the phoenix rise above its own ashes.

I would have you consider your judgment and your appetite even as you would two loved guests in your house.

Surely you would not honour one guest above the other; for he who is more mindful of one loses the love and the faith of both.

Among the hills, when you sit in the cool shade of the white poplars, sharing the peace and serenity of distant fields and meadows—then let your heart say in silence, "God rests in reason."

And when the storm comes, and the mighty wind shakes the forest, and thunder and lightning proclaim the majesty of the sky,—then let your heart say in awe, "God moves in passion."

And since you are a breath in God's sphere, and a leaf in God's forest, you too should rest in reason and move in passion.

nd a woman spoke, saying, Tell us of Pain.

And he said:

Your pain is the breaking of the shell that en-
closes your understanding.

Even as the stone of the fruit must break, that its heart
may stand in the sun, so must you know pain.

And could you keep your heart in wonder at the daily
miracles of your life, your pain would not seem less won-
drous than your joy;

And you would accept the seasons of your heart, even
as you have always accepted the seasons that pass over
your fields.

And you would watch with serenity through the win-
ters of your grief.

Much of your pain is self-chosen.

It is the bitter potion by which the physician within
you heals your sick self.

Therefore trust the physician, and drink his remedy in
silence and tranquillity:

For his hand, though heavy and hard, is guided by the
tender hand of the Unseen,

And the cup he brings, though it burn your lips, has
been fashioned of the clay which the Potter has moist-
ened with His own sacred tears.

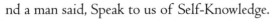 nd a man said, Speak to us of Self-Knowledge.

And he answered, saying:

Your hearts know in silence the secrets of the days and the nights.

But your ears thirst for the sound of your heart's knowledge.

You would know in words that which you have always known in thought.

You would touch with your fingers the naked body of your dreams.

And it is well you should.

The hidden well-spring of your soul must needs rise and run murmuring to the sea;

And the treasure of your infinite depths would be revealed to your eyes.

But let there be no scales to weigh your unknown treasure;

And seek not the depths of your knowledge with staff or sounding line.

For self is a sea boundless and measureless.

Say not, "I have found the truth," but rather, "I have found a truth."

Say not, "I have found the path of the soul."

Say rather, "I have met the soul walking upon my path."

For the soul walks upon all paths.

The soul walks not upon a line, neither does it grow like a reed.

The soul unfolds itself, like a lotus of countless petals.

hen said a teacher, Speak to us of Teaching.

And he said:

"No man can reveal to you aught but that which already lies half asleep in the dawning of your knowledge.

The teacher who walks in the shadow of the temple, among his followers, gives not of his wisdom but rather of his faith and his lovingness.

If he is indeed wise he does not bid you enter the house of his wisdom, but rather leads you to the threshold of your own mind.

The astronomer may speak to you of his understanding of space, but he cannot give you his understanding.

The musician may sing to you of the rhythm which is in all space, but he cannot give you the ear which arrests the rhythm nor the voice that echoes it.

And he who is versed in the science of numbers can tell of the regions of weight and measure, but he cannot conduct you thither.

For the vision of one man lends not its wings to another man.

And even as each one of you stands alone in God's knowledge, so must each one of you be alone in his knowledge of God and in his understanding of the earth.

nd a youth said, Speak to us of Friendship.

And he answered, saying:

Your friend is your needs answered.

He is your field which you sow with love and reap with thanksgiving.

And he is your board and your fireside.

For you come to him with your hunger, and you seek him for peace.

When your friend speaks his mind you fear not the "nay" in your own mind, nor do you withhold the "ay."

And when he is silent your heart ceases not to listen to his heart;

For without words, in friendship, all thoughts, all desires, all expectations are born and shared, with joy that is unacclaimed.

When you part from your friend, you grieve not;

For that which you love most in him may be clearer in his absence, as the mountain to the climber is clearer from the plain.

And let there be no purpose in friendship save the deepening of the spirit.

For love that seeks aught but the disclosure of its own mystery is not love but a net cast forth: and only the unprofitable is caught.

And let your best be for your friend.

If he must know the ebb of your tide, let him know its flood also.

For what is your friend that you should seek him with hours to kill?

Seek him always with hours to live.

For it is his to fill your need, but not your emptiness.

And in the sweetness of friendship let there be laughter, and sharing of pleasures.

For in the dew of little things the heart finds its morning and is refreshed.

And then a scholar said, Speak of Talking.

And he answered, saying:

You talk when you cease to be at peace with your thoughts;

And when you can no longer dwell in the solitude of your heart you live in your lips, and sound is a diversion and a pastime.

And in much of your talking, thinking is half murdered.

For thought is a bird of space, that in a cage of words may indeed unfold its wings but cannot fly.

There are those among you who seek the talkative through fear of being alone.

The silence of aloneness reveals to their eyes their naked selves and they would escape.

And there are those who talk, and without knowledge or forethought reveal a truth which they themselves do not understand.

And there are those who have the truth within them, but they tell it not in words.

In the bosom of such as these the spirit dwells in rhythmic silence.

When you meet your friend on the roadside or in the market place, let the spirit in you move your lips and direct your tongue.

Let the voice within your voice speak to the ear of his
ear;

For his soul will keep the truth of your heart as the
taste of the wine is remembered

When the colour is forgotten and the vessel is no more.

nd an astronomer said, Master, what of Time?

And he answered:

You would measure time the measureless and the immeasurable.

You would adjust your conduct and even direct the course of your spirit according to hours and seasons.

Of time you would make a stream upon whose bank you would sit and watch its flowing.

Yet the timeless in you is aware of life's timelessness,

And knows that yesterday is but today's memory and tomorrow is today's dream.

And that that which sings and contemplates in you is still dwelling within the bounds of that first moment which scattered the stars into space.

Who among you does not feel that his power to love is boundless?

And yet who does not feel that very love, though boundless, encompassed within the centre of his being, and moving not from love thought to love thought, nor from love deeds to other love deeds?

And is not time even as love is, undivided and paceless?

But if in your thought you must measure time into seasons, let each season encircle all the other seasons,

And let today embrace the past with remembrance and the future with longing.

And one of the elders of the city said, Speak to us of Good and Evil.

And he answered:

Of the good in you I can speak, but not of the evil.

For what is evil but good tortured by its own hunger and thirst?

Verily when good is hungry it seeks food even in dark caves, and when it thirsts it drinks even of dead waters.

You are good when you are one with yourself.

Yet when you are not one with yourself you are not evil.

For a divided house is not a den of thieves; it is only a divided house.

And a ship without rudder may wander aimlessly among perilous isles yet sink not to the bottom.

You are good when you strive to give of yourself.

Yet you are not evil when you seek gain for yourself.

For when you strive for gain you are but a root that clings to the earth and sucks at her breast.

Surely the fruit cannot say to the root, "Be like me, ripe and full and ever giving of your abundance."

For to the fruit giving is a need, as receiving is a need to the root.

You are good when you are fully awake in your speech,

Yet you are not evil when you sleep while your tongue staggers without purpose.

And even stumbling speech may strengthen a weak tongue.

You are good when you walk to your goal firmly and with bold steps.

Yet you are not evil when you go thither limping.

Even those who limp go not backward.

But you who are strong and swift, see that you do not limp before the lame, deeming it kindness.

You are good in countless ways, and you are not evil when you are not good,

You are only loitering and sluggard.

Pity that the stags cannot teach swiftness to the turtles.

In your longing for your giant self lies your goodness: and that longing is in all of you.

But in some of you that longing is a torrent rushing with might to the sea, carrying the secrets of the hillsides and the songs of the forest.

And in others it is a flat stream that loses itself in angles and bends and lingers before it reaches the shore.

But let not him who longs much say to him who longs little, "Wherefore are you slow and halting?"

For the truly good ask not the naked, "Where is your garment?" nor the houseless, "What has befallen your house?"

hen a priestess said, Speak to us of Prayer.

And he answered, saying:

You pray in your distress and in your need; would that you might pray also in the fullness of your joy and in your days of abundance.

For what is prayer but the expansion of yourself into the living ether?

And if it is for your comfort to pour your darkness into space, it is also for your delight to pour forth the dawning of your heart.

And if you cannot but weep when your soul summons you to prayer, she should spur you again and yet again, though weeping, until you shall come laughing.

When you pray you rise to meet in the air those who are praying at that very hour, and whom save in prayer you may not meet.

Therefore let your visit to that temple invisible be for naught but ecstasy and sweet communion.

For if you should enter the temple for no other purpose than asking you shall not receive:

And if you should enter into it to humble yourself you shall not be lifted:

Or even if you should enter into it to beg for the good of others you shall not be heard.

It is enough that you enter the temple invisible.

I cannot teach you how to pray in words.

God listens not to your words save when He Himself utters them through your lips.

And I cannot teach you the prayer of the seas and the forests and the mountains. But you who are born of the mountains and the forests and the seas can find their prayer in your heart,

And if you but listen in the stillness of the night you shall hear them saying in silence,

"Our God, who art our winged self, it is thy will in us that willeth.

It is thy desire in us that desireth.

It is thy urge in us that would turn our nights, which are thine, into days which are thine also.

We cannot ask thee for aught, for thou knowest our needs before they are born in us:

Thou art our need; and in giving us more of thyself thou givest us all."

Then a hermit, who visited the city once a year, came forth and said, Speak to us of Pleasure.

And he answered, saying:

Pleasure is a freedom-song,

But it is not freedom.

It is the blossoming of your desires,

But it is not their fruit.

It is a depth calling unto a height,

But it is not the deep nor the high.

It is the caged taking wing,

But it is not space encompassed.

Ay, in very truth, pleasure is a freedom-song.

And I fain would have you sing it with fullness of heart; yet I would not have you lose your hearts in the singing.

Some of your youth seek pleasure as if it were all, and they are judged and rebuked. I would not judge nor rebuke them. I would have them seek.

For they shall find pleasure, but not her alone;

Seven are her sisters, and the least of them is more beautiful than pleasure.

Have you not heard of the man who was digging in the earth for roots and found a treasure?

And some of your elders remember pleasures with regret like wrongs committed in drunkenness.

But regret is the beclouding of the mind and not its chastisement.

They should remember their pleasures with gratitude, as they would the harvest of a summer.

Yet if it comforts them to regret, let them be comforted.

And there are among you those who are neither young to seek nor old to remember;

And in their fear of seeking and remembering they shun all pleasures, lest they neglect the spirit or offend against it.

But even in their foregoing is their pleasure.

And thus they too find a treasure though they dig for roots with quivering hands.

But tell me, who is he that can offend the spirit?

Shall the nightingale offend the stillness of the night, or the firefly the stars?

And shall your flame or your smoke burden the wind?

Think you the spirit is a still pool which you can trouble with a staff?

Oftentimes in denying yourself pleasure you do but store the desire in the recesses of your being.

Who knows but that which seems omitted today, waits for tomorrow?

Even your body knows its heritage and its rightful need and will not be deceived.

And your body is the harp of your soul,

And it is yours to bring forth sweet music from it or confused sounds.

And now you ask in your heart, "How shall we distinguish that which is good in pleasure from that which is not good?"

Go to your fields and your gardens, and you shall learn that it is the pleasure of the bee to gather honey of the flower,

But it is also the pleasure of the flower to yield its honey to the bee.

For to the bee a flower is a fountain of life,

And to the flower a bee is a messenger of love,

And to both, bee and flower, the giving and the receiving of pleasure is a need and an ecstasy.

People of Orphalese, be in your pleasures like the flowers and the bees.

nd a poet said, Speak to us of Beauty.

And he answered:

Where shall you seek beauty, and how shall you find her unless she herself be your way and your guide?

And how shall you speak of her except she be the weaver of your speech?

The aggrieved and the injured say, "Beauty is kind and gentle.

Like a young mother half-shy of her own glory she walks among us."

And the passionate say, "Nay, beauty is a thing of might and dread.

Like the tempest she shakes the earth beneath us and the sky above us."

The tired and the weary say, "Beauty is of soft whisperings. She speaks in our spirit. Her voice yields to our silences like a faint light that quivers in fear of the shadow."

But the restless say, "We have heard her shouting among the mountains,

And with her cries came the sound of hoofs, and the beating of wings and the roaring of lions."

At night the watchmen of the city say, "Beauty shall rise with the dawn from the east."

And at noontide the toilers and the wayfarers say, "We have seen her leaning over the earth from the windows of the sunset."

In winter say the snow-bound, "She shall come with the spring leaping upon the hills."

And in the summer heat the reapers say, "We have seen her dancing with the autumn leaves, and we saw a drift of snow in her hair."

All these things have you said of beauty,

Yet in truth you spoke not of her but of needs unsatisfied,

And beauty is not a need but an ecstasy.

It is not a mouth thirsting nor an empty hand stretched forth,

But rather a heart enflamed and a soul enchanted.

It is not the image you would see nor the song you would hear,

But rather an image you see though you close your eyes and a song you hear though you shut your ears.

It is not the sap within the furrowed bark, nor a wing attached to a claw,

But rather a garden for ever in bloom and a flock of angels for ever in flight.

People of Orphalese, beauty is life when life unveils her holy face.

But you are life and you are the veil.

Beauty is eternity gazing at itself in a mirror.

But you are eternity and you are the mirror.

nd an old priest said, Speak to us of Religion.

And he said:

Have I spoken this day of aught else?

Is not religion all deeds and all reflection,

And that which is neither deed nor reflection, but a wonder and a surprise ever springing in the soul, even while the hands hew the stone or tend the loom?

Who can separate his faith from his actions, or his belief from his occupations?

Who can spread his hours before him, saying, "This for God and this for myself; This for my soul, and this other for my body?"

All your hours are wings that beat through space from self to self.

He who wears his morality but as his best garment were better naked.

The wind and the sun will tear no holes in his skin.

And he who defines his conduct by ethics imprisons his song-bird in a cage.

The freest song comes not through bars and wires.

And he to whom worshipping is a window, to open but also to shut, has not yet visited the house of his soul whose windows are from dawn to dawn.

Your daily life is your temple and your religion.

Whenever you enter into it take with you your all.

Take the plough and the forge and the mallet and the lute,

The things you have fashioned in necessity or for delight.

For in revery you cannot rise above your achievements nor fall lower than your failures.

And take with you all men: For in adoration you cannot fly higher than their hopes nor humble yourself lower than their despair.

And if you would know God be not therefore a solver of riddles.

Rather look about you and you shall see Him playing with your children.

And look into space; you shall see Him walking in the cloud, outstretching His arms in the lightning and descending in rain.

You shall see Him smiling in flowers, then rising and waving His hands in trees.

Then Almitra spoke, saying, We would ask now of Death.

And he said:

You would know the secret of death.

But how shall you find it unless you seek it in the heart of life?

The owl whose night-bound eyes are blind unto the day cannot unveil the mystery of light.

If you would indeed behold the spirit of death, open your heart wide unto the body of life.

For life and death are one, even as the river and the sea are one.

In the depth of your hopes and desires lies your silent knowledge of the beyond;

And like seeds dreaming beneath the snow your heart dreams of spring.

Trust the dreams, for in them is hidden the gate to eternity.

Your fear of death is but the trembling of the shepherd when he stands before the king whose hand is to be laid upon him in honour.

Is the shepherd not joyful beneath his trembling, that he shall wear the mark of the king?

Yet is he not more mindful of his trembling?

For what is it to die but to stand naked in the wind and to melt into the sun?

And what is it to cease breathing, but to free the breath from its restless tides, that it may rise and expand and seek God unencumbered?

Only when you drink from the river of silence shall you indeed sing.

And when you have reached the mountain top, then you shall begin to climb.

And when the earth shall claim your limbs, then shall you truly dance.

nd now it was evening.

And Almitra the seeress said, Blessed be this day and this place and your spirit that has spoken.

And he answered, Was it I who spoke? Was I not also a listener?

Then he descended the steps of the Temple and all the people followed him. And he reached his ship and stood upon the deck.

And facing the people again, he raised his voice and said:

People of Orphalese, the wind bids me leave you.

Less hasty am I than the wind, yet I must go.

We wanderers, ever seeking the lonelier way, begin no day where we have ended another day; and no sunrise finds us where sunset left us.

Even while the earth sleeps we travel.

We are the seeds of the tenacious plant, and it is in our ripeness and our fullness of heart that we are given to the wind and are scattered.

Brief were my days among you, and briefer still the words I have spoken.

But should my voice fade in your ears, and my love vanish in your memory, then I will come again,

And with a richer heart and lips more yielding to the spirit will I speak.

Yea, I shall return with the tide,

And though death may hide me, and the greater silence enfold me, yet again will I seek your understanding.

And not in vain will I seek.

If aught I have said is truth, that truth shall reveal itself in a clearer voice, and in words more kin to your thoughts.

I go with the wind, people of Orphalese, but not down into emptiness;

And if this day is not a fulfilment of your needs and my love, then let it be a promise till another day.

Man's needs change, but not his love, nor his desire that his love should satisfy his needs.

Know therefore, that from the greater silence I shall return.

The mist that drifts away at dawn, leaving but dew in the fields, shall rise and gather into a cloud and then fall down in rain.

And not unlike the the mist have I been.

In the stillness of the night I have walked in your streets, and my spirit has entered your houses,

And your heart-beats were in my heart, and your breath was upon my face, and I knew you all.

Ay, I knew your joy and your pain, and in your sleep your dreams were my dreams.

And oftentimes I was among you a lake among the mountains.

I mirrored the summits in you and the bending slopes, and even the passing flocks of your thoughts and your desires.

And to my silence came the laughter of your children in streams, and the longing of your youths in rivers.

And when they reached my depth the streams and the rivers ceased not yet to sing.

But sweeter still than laughter and greater than longing came to me.

It was the boundless in you;

The vast man in whom you are all but cells and sinews;

He in whose chant all your singing is but a soundless throbbing.

It is in the vast man that you are vast,

And in beholding him that I beheld you and loved you.

For what distances can love reach that are not in that vast sphere?

What visions, what expectations and what presumptions can outsoar that flight?

Like a giant oak tree covered with apple blossoms is the vast man in you.

His might binds you to the earth, his fragrance lifts you into space, and in his durability you are deathless.

You have been told that, even like a chain, you are as weak as your weakest link.

This is but half the truth. You are also as strong as your strongest link.

To measure you by your smallest deed is to reckon the power of ocean by the frailty of its foam.

To judge you by your failures is to cast blame upon the seasons for their inconstancy.

Ay, you are like an ocean,

And though heavy-grounded ships await the tide upon your shores, yet, even like an ocean, you cannot hasten your tides.

And like the seasons you are also,

And though in your winter you deny your spring,

Yet spring, reposing within you, smiles in her drowsiness and is not offended.

Think not I say these things in order that you may say the one to the other, "He praised us well. He saw but the good in us."

I only speak to you in words of that which you yourselves know in thought.

And what is word knowledge but a shadow of wordless knowledge?

Your thoughts and my words are waves from a sealed memory that keeps records of our yesterdays,

And of the ancient days when the earth knew not us nor herself,

And of nights when earth was up-wrought with confusion.

Wise men have come to you to give you of their wisdom. I came to take of your wisdom:

And behold I have found that which is greater than wisdom.

It is a flame spirit in you ever gathering more of itself, While you, heedless of its expansion, bewail the withering of your days.

It is life in quest of life in bodies that fear the grave.

There are no graves here.

These mountains and plains are a cradle and a stepping-stone.

Whenever you pass by the field where you have laid your ancestors look well thereupon, and you shall see yourselves and your children dancing hand in hand.

Verily you often make merry without knowing.

Others have come to you to whom for golden promises made unto your faith you have given but riches and power and glory.

Less than a promise have I given, and yet more generous have you been to me.

You have given me my deeper thirsting after life.

Surely there is no greater gift to a man than that which turns all his aims into parching lips and all life into a fountain.

And in this lies my honour and my reward,—

That whenever I come to the fountain to drink I find the living water itself thirsty;
And it drinks me while I drink it.

Some of you have deemed me proud and over-shy to receive gifts.
Too proud indeed am I to receive wages, but not gifts.
And though I have eaten berries among the hills when you would have had me sit at your board,
And slept in the portico of the temple when you would gladly have sheltered me,
Yet was it not your loving mindfulness of my days and my nights that made food sweet to my mouth and girdled my sleep with visions?

For this I bless you most:
You give much and know not that you give at all.
Verily the kindness that gazes upon itself in a mirror turns to stone,
And a good deed that calls itself by tender names becomes the parent to a curse.

And some of you have called me aloof, and drunk with my own aloneness,

And you have said, "He holds council with the trees of the forest, but not with men.

He sits alone on hill-tops and looks down upon our city."

True it is that I have climbed the hills and walked in remote places.

How could I have seen you save from a great height or a great distance?

How can one be indeed near unless he be far?

And others among you called unto me, not in words, and they said,

"Stranger, stranger, lover of unreachable heights, why dwell you among the summits where eagles build their nests?

Why seek you the unattainable?

What storms would you trap in your net,

And what vaporous birds do you hunt in the sky?

Come and be one of us.

Descend and appease your hunger with our bread and quench your thirst with our wine."

In the solitude of their souls they said these things;

But were their solitude deeper they would have known that I sought but the secret of your joy and your pain,

And I hunted only your larger selves that walk the sky.

But the hunter was also the hunted;

For many of my arrows left my bow only to seek my own breast.

And the flier was also the creeper;

For when my wings were spread in the sun their shadow upon the earth was a turtle.

And I the believer was also the doubter;

For often have I put my finger in my own wound that I might have the greater belief in you and the greater knowledge of you.

And it is with this belief and this knowledge that I say,

You are not enclosed within your bodies, nor confined to houses or fields.

That which is you dwells above the mountain and roves with the wind.

It is not a thing that crawls into the sun for warmth or digs holes into darkness for safety,

But a thing free, a spirit that envelops the earth and moves in the ether.

If these be vague words, then seek not to clear them.

Vague and nebulous is the beginning of all things, but not their end,

And I fain would have you remember me as a beginning.

Life, and all that lives, is conceived in the mist and not in the crystal.

And who knows but a crystal is mist in decay?

This would I have you remember in remembering me:

That which seems most feeble and bewildered in you is the strongest and most determined.

Is it not your breath that has erected and hardened the structure of your bones?

And is it not a dream which none of you remember having dreamt, that builded your city and fashioned all there is in it?

Could you but see the tides of that breath you would cease to see all else,

And if you could hear the whispering of the dream you would hear no other sound.

But you do not see, nor do you hear, and it is well.

The veil that clouds your eyes shall be lifted by the hands that wove it,

And the clay that fills your ears shall be pierced by those fingers that kneaded it.

And you shall see.

And you shall hear.

Yet you shall not deplore having known blindness, nor regret having been deaf.

For in that day you shall know the hidden purposes in all things,

And you shall bless darkness as you would bless light.

After saying these things he looked about him, and he saw the pilot of his ship standing by the helm and gazing now at the full sails and now at the distance.

And he said:

Patient, over patient, is the captain of my ship.

The wind blows, and restless are the sails;

Even the rudder begs direction;

Yet quietly my captain awaits my silence.

And these my mariners, who have heard the choir of the greater sea, they too have heard me patiently.

Now they shall wait no longer.

I am ready.

The stream has reached the sea, and once more the great mother holds her son against her breast.

Fare you well, people of Orphalese.

This day has ended.

It is closing upon us even as the water-lily upon its own tomorrow.

What was given us here we shall keep,

And if it suffices not, then again must we come together and together stretch our hands unto the giver.

Forget not that I shall come back to you.

A little while, and my longing shall gather dust and foam for another body.

A little while, a moment of rest upon the wind, and another woman shall bear me.

Farewell to you and the youth I have spent with you.

It was but yesterday we met in a dream.

You have sung to me in my aloneness, and I of your longings have built a tower in the sky.

But now our sleep has fled and our dream is over, and it is no longer dawn.

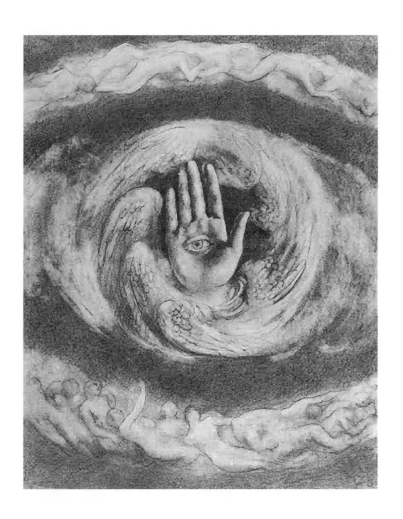

The noontide is upon us and our half waking has turned to fuller day, and we must part.

If in the twilight of memory we should meet once more, we shall speak again together and you shall sing to me a deeper song.

And if our hands should meet in another dream we shall build another tower in the sky.

So saying he made a signal to the seamen, and straight-way they weighed anchor and cast the ship loose from its moorings, and they moved eastward.

And a cry came from the people as from a single heart, and it rose into the dusk and was carried out over the sea like a great trumpeting.

Only Almitra was silent, gazing after the ship until it had vanished into the mist.

And when all the people were dispersed she still stood alone upon the sea-wall, remembering in her heart his saying,

"A little while, a moment of rest upon the wind, and another woman shall bear me."

Part Two

Poems

The Waterfall

We Came as a Mist

(Undated, translated from his own Arabic)

And now I say unto you,
Beloved, seek us no more,
For we have neither hut nor bower,
And search not for our name
For it is neither written in books
Nor is it traced on any canvas.

We came as a mist.
We passed away as a cloud,
The one, without dew,
The other without rain.
And now if you would in truth know what we have
   known,
You must needs walk the road to death
Even as we have walked.

FRAGMENTS

(Undated)

Heart of my ancient race, in whose heart my race dwells
   in majesty,
To you I bring my pride, wounded, yet proud.
And at your feet I lay my staff.
And at your door my journeying finds an end,
And my dreams a beginning.

Too long have I wandered in alien lands,
And too far have I walked with the sons and daughters
   of alien tribes.
It was your light that turned my inversed eyes,
And it was my mist that led me back,
And it was that veil that made things fair.
It was my dream that sought dreams where naught exists
   but mockery.
It was a hunger that would pluck a fruit,
A thirst that would hold a cup.
And now I return to you, not a conqueror, yet not
   conquered.
Only a man made a stranger by his own yielding,
Wiser by his own youth,
More faithful by his own crushed faith.

Heart of my ancient race,
In whose heart my race dwells in majesty,
I have come back to you!

Untitled

(Undated)

Now let us sing of her loveliness.

Of the loveliness of her who is dead and no more
returning.

She gazed lovingly upon the day,

And the night gazed lovingly upon her face.

And even she of great loveliness,

She was wrapped in linen

And like all others carried in a coffin

To the high-towered church,

And from the church carried to the ancient burial
ground.

And people followed her body.

And I was the last one following.

But no man knew that two were dead,

One in a coffin, and the other the last to follow.

Now let us sing of her loveliness,

Of the loveliness of her who is dead

And no more returning.

Untitled

(Undated)

I went up the hill
With bread and wine,
And ate my loaf
And drank my cup.
Then I was drowsy
And slept in the sun.
And as I slept
A lark came down
And picked a crumb
Out of my hand;
And drank a drop
From upon my lip.
And then he flew
Into the air,
And fluttered his wings,
And sang his song.
And waked my heart
And opened my eyes.

Then said I,
Would that he had
All the bread
Upon my hand,

And all the wine
Within my heart.
For all there is
In hand and heart
Would rise and sing.

Pity it is
We drowse too soon;
Pity it is
We fall asleep
Ere our song
Encompass the height,
And ere our hand
Inherit the deep.

UNTITLED

(Undated. Editor's Note: incomplete, as found)

I took you to my mother's house and loved you. In the chamber where she gave me birth I kissed and comforted you. With my mother's ancient jewels I adorned your head and bosom, and with love-woven garments I covered your body.

I took you into my mother's house and before the silvery mirror which reflected her thousand tender countenances I enthroned you and made you sit and smile at your own youth. I took you into my mother's house and loved you. I loved you even with a father's love though my years were but equal unto yours. And I loved you with a brother's love even as if we had drunk life from the [same] breasts.

And in the high hours of the night I was your husband; and in the deep hour of dawn I was your babe.

I took you into my mother's house and loved you. But when I left you for a day and a night and went forth to conquer your father's enemy, and to erase the same from your father's house, then did you love a slave.

From my mother's window, and with your hand adorned with my mother's jewels, did you beckon to my mother's slave, and in her sacred bed you gave yourself to him.

O serpent woman! O she-wolf! It was your cursed mother clad in your young flesh that came to my mother's house.

I took her to my mother's house and loved her. In the chamber in which my mother gave me birth, I kissed and comforted her. With my mother's ancient jewels I adorned her head and bosom, and with love-woven garments I covered her body.

I took her into my mother's house, and before the silvery mirror

THE OTHER PERSON

(Undated)

You say I am of the spirit;

It is true, for I am of the earth.
You say I know God;
It is true, for I know man.

You would anoint me and crown me king,
And I would be anointed and crowned.
For a leper am I, and a beggar at your door.

You would raise me beyond my dreams,
And I would yield, for when I sleep and dream,
I sleep at your feet;
Fore there dawn lingers forever,
And there I will find my soul.

THE SACRED VINE

(Undated)

The grape is a jewel.
The leaves are jewels.
The fragrance is amber.
The taste is desire poured into a cup.
Should a lover drink
He would be lost in wonder,
And deem it his own love
Running,
A stream from his lips to his heart.

SILENCE

(Undated)

Ah, this silence of my soul
That was when my soul was riding the wind;
This silence that was a leader and a guardian

But when my soul descended
And builded a house of earth and dew,
She gazed, and there was silence,
A next-door neighbor,
And at times a constant guest
Sleeping she sleeps, with my soul
Rising when she rises
Walking the fields with her,
And resting close at even-tide.
There is no escape even in dreams
Nor is there a lonely path in daylight.

When my soul speaks silence clings betwixt her tongue
and her lips.
When she sings
Silence is her voice,
The high and the low.

And when she lives a day,
And would reveal its beauty,
Silence is the master-revealer.
And from her he would veil
Even her own secret,
As though she were a charge,
And he her keeper appointed.

How often had she begged him for a moment of
    aloneness
That she may fill the corners of the earth
With her tales.

Yet she was driven by him in the beginning
Against her wings.

And now—he drives the hidden thing in her
But with her will
But my silence is a song
And in his hunger I am satisfied.

I know no thirst,
For in this sober thing you see
Is God's intoxicated touch.

I lament,
But there is a wedding feast in my lamentation.

I am a stranger in a strange land,
But whenever I lift up my head and gaze
I find my own people.

And whenever I tear my garment
I find a breast.

And though I walk, alone and wordless,
The streets of an alien city,
Yet I am a marching regiment
Shouting in victory.

I have often bewailed a sorrow,
But more often I have been too proud of that sorrow
To yield it to a joy.

And I have wept,
While my lips made smiling sport of tears.

Once I gazed at my body in a mirror,
And I saw naught but spirit,
Confined and wingless.

And once I listened
When my desires conversed one with the other,
And their speech was like distant lights revealed by night
Dispelled by dawn.

And I often have longed for my beloved,
When my beloved was lying close unto me.

And sought after power
When it was but a glittering thing
Crying within my hand.

Now I know

That here within me is mine own maker,
Even he, the builder of my roads and bridges.
And here upon my bed
Lie life and death and the forevermore.
And they lie in silence.

It is dawn now.
I say to my soul, "Answer this:
What shall time do with your hunger, thirst, longing
Even with your silence?"

And she answered, "Gaze and see my face.
I am time.
If you were not in life
You would think not of death.
And if there were not a throne sought
You would seek no grave."

BRIDE OF MY DREAMS

(March 1931. Editor's Note: "The Bride of my Dreams" was the last poem translated by Kahlil prior to his death)

Whence, Bride of my dreams?
Go hence slowly, Bride of my deeper dream,
For I am now weary afoot,
And I cannot follow.
. . .

Go fast, faster, Bride of my dreams,
For the valleys and the high hills
I feared but yesterday,
Now I would cross and climb.

Go fast, faster. I follow.
My spirit is ready and I would run.
Fly, Bride of my dreams,
For there are wings springing upon my shoulders.
The flame that I feared of burning now I embrace,
For I would be enflamed;
And now I would bathe only at the high tide of the sea.

It was at the Autumn of my years
That I beheld you in the mist.
Now it is Spring, Bride of my dreams.

Run fast, fly high.
I follow.

Let Me Be with Love

(Undated)

Let me be with love
Going toward the eve of my days.
Let me be with love
Whilst you are passioning toward your hopes,
Whist I fold in the roads of my dreams.
And let me now listen
To songs you will not hear—
You will not hear.

If your songs are in your days,
My choir is in my night.
Let me be with love,
For who amongst you knows
When night challenges me,
And is there one upon this street save love
Who would meet night with me?

Let me be with this ancient ache.
My physician is beyond the sky,
And my medicine is of the ether,
Farewell to you.

NIGHTMARE

(Undated)

You saw me standing upon the banks of the river
Adonis, a man with a lyre and a song.

Your eyes were filled and your ears were drunk with
song, and the soul within you danced with promised
delight.

Then you said in your silence, "This man shall be my
lover. In his heart I shall find a tower to house my fuller
thoughts; and of his cupped hands I shall make a vessel
for the wine of my ripened years, and I shall be at peace
in his strength; and I shall not [hunger] nor shall I know
thirst in his fruit-laden garden."

And you approached me, and with the reflected glow of
your younger days, and with lips trembling in ecstasy
half-certain of itself, you spoke to me and said:

"Of all the men that stand on the bank of my river, you
alone I love, and your face is the face of my dream, and
your song I hear my own god chanting. And if you but lay
your hand upon my breast I would indeed rejoice before
the sun, and like sweet prayer I shall follow your path."

And I believed your words for I too was weary of
aloneness, and the voices in me were longing for
ears, and the secret treasures in me would seek your
knowledge.

And you were glad with the gladness of April, and
you wept for joy. And I held your face with my hands
and gazed into your eyes even as my ancient brother in
Ninevah gazed into a crystal.

When night came you led me to your house, and I like
a child who knew naught but his own holy needs I sat at
your table and I ate your bread and I drank your wine.

And then I slept, naked guiless and disarmed.

And as I lay embracing my dreams a creature half
woman and half beast rose like a black cloud form your
bosom, and held me by the throat.

And as I wrestled with her I looked at her face and I
beheld your countenance.

Then I woke with a cry, and I found you asleep, and
upon your lips a smile and upon your closed eyes a veil
of serenity.

On earth, forever green and white, in your longing you
have hunted me in the sky,

And now in my awakening I know it was your love
seeking love

Yet in my sleep I am not here, I am not with you,

And I see but that other face.

Forgive me awhile.

THE BEAUTY OF DEATH

(1908. Originally entitled "Death Beautiful")

I

Let me swoon into sleep, for I am drowned/intoxicated
  (drenched) with love.

Let me rest, for love has fed one day and night.

Light the candles, burn the incense around my bed;

Strew me with leaves of narcissus and rose;

Sweeten my hair with powder of musk;

With fragrant oil anoint my feet;

Look in my eyes there, son of my mother.

And see what the hand of Death writes on my forehead.

Life has

Let the dawns of slumber

Enfold me darkly

Close my eyes

Filled/sated with the vision of this life.

For my eyes, sated with this vision, would fain close.

Sound the lyre

With unshaken hand now

Strike the lyre

Let its gold chords sing in my ear and sleep with me.

Let flutes and pipes breathe forth a mist to envelope my
  heart

That runs to its rest.

Sing the song of Rahowi the land whence divine songs
come

And make of their meaning

Than

A bed for my numbed senses

Look in my eyes and see the rays of hope.

Dry your tears, companions of my youth.

Raise up your heads like flowers at dawn

And see my bride death

A pillar of light standing

Between my bed and the immeasurable gloom.

Hold your breath an instant and hear her silken wings.

Came for leave-taking, O Children of my mother.

Kiss my forehead with smiling lips—kiss my lips with
your eyelids—my eyelids with your lips

Bring the children near my bed.

With fingers of rose to caress my throat

Let the

Bring the aged come here to bless my forehead with
their withered hands.

Call the daughters of meadows and field to see the
shadow of the unknown pass under my brows and
catch in my last breath the echo of infinity.

II.

Lo, I have reached the summit and the spirit who is I
  has soared into a heaven of freedom.

I am far far O Sons of Mother Earth

Mist veils the hillsides

The hillsides are mist-veiled

Misty are the hillsides veiled

The valleys and the fields sunk/drowned in a sea of
  silence

The meadows, the ridges, the slopes, dissolve at the
  touch of the finger of my flight.

Sea, Forests and deserts glimmer

Faintly beyond the river of souls,

White as spring clouds, yellow as sunlight and red as
  veil of sunset

multitudes, white, sunny red lucent shimmering souls

The songs of oceans are silent beat against the silence
  below me.

The air beyond and silence against which the songs of
  ocean break. And I hear naught save the

hymn of eternity. Which is the everlasting voice of the
  unknown.

I have outstripped the cries of men

The voice I hear is the hymn of Eternity—the
  everlasting unknown.

Rest

Take off the linen shroud—lay me in lilies

From the ivory coffin lift me to pillows of orange
   blossoms

Wail not, youths, but sing of your youth and your joy.

Sing O Maidens of the field and vineyard

The song of the grapes and the wheat sheaves

No sighs O'er my breast but the love-sign rings,
   described by love's fingers

BE STILL MY HEART

(Undated)

Be still, my heart, for space does not hear you,

For the air which is heavy with mourning cannot carry
your songs.

Be still, my heart, for the phantoms of the night are
heedless of the whispers of your secret,

And the hosts of darkness will not stop for your
dreams.

Be still, my heart, until dawn,

For he who awaits patiently for dawn will find dawn

And he who loves light will be loved by light.

Be still, my heart, and hear what I have to say.

In my dream I saw a thrush singing above the mouth of
a raging volcano;

And I saw also a lily lift its head above the snow,

And I saw a naked houri dance in a graveyard.

And I saw a babe toss skulls about, while it laughed
aloud;

All these things I saw in my dreams, and I did not
awake.

And I looked about me, and I saw the volcano in fury,

But I could not hear nor see the thrush flutter about.

And I saw the snows sprinkle snow upon the valleys and
the dales
Concealing with its white shroud the silent lily.
And I saw the graves, row upon row, in the face of the
silence of ages.
But not a single person dancing or praying upon a grave.
And I saw there a heap of skulls, but naught smiled
there with but the wind.
When awake I saw sorrow and grief,
But where, but where have the joys of dreams gone?
Where is gone the light of sleep, and how has its image
vanished?
Be still, my heart, and listen to my words.
My soul yesterday was an old strong tree,
The roots of which had penetrated deep into the earth,
The branches of which had reached into eternity.
And my soul blossomed in Spring, and bore fruit in
Summer.
And then when Autumn came I gathered the fruit on
trays of silver, and placed them at the crossroads,
And the passersby reached for them and ate, and went
their way.
And when Autumn had passed and its jubilation was
converted into grief,
I looked and saw upon my tray only a single fruit which
was left for me.

The Struggle

And I took it and ate of it, and found it bitter as aloes,
and sour as green grapes.

Then I said to myself, "Woe is me, for I have placed in
the mouth of my fellows a curse,

And hostility in their bowels."

What then, my soul, have you done with that sweetness
which your roots had imbibed from the bosom of
earth?

"And with that incense which your branches had drunk
from the rays of the sun?"

So, I uprooted the strong, old tree of my soul;

I plucked its very roots from the soil where it grew and
prospered,

And I severed it from its past and dismantled it of
the memory of a thousand Springs and a thousand
Autumns,

And I planted the tree of my soul in another spot.

I planted it in a field far away from the path of time,

And through the night I would stay awake beneath it,
saying,

"To be awake together brings us nearer to the stars."

And I watered it with my tears and gave it my blood to
drink, saying

"There is a fragrance in blood and a sweetness in tears."

And when Spring came again my soul blossomed once
more, and in Summer it bore fruit.

And when Autumn was close I gathered the ripe fruit on
trays of gold and placed them at the crossroads,
And men passed by, but not one reached a hand to take
the fruit.

So, I took a fruit and ate, and found it as sweet as
honey, luscious as nectar, and fragrant as the breath
of jasmine.

And I cried aloud and said, "Men would not have a
blessing in their mouths nor feel the truth in their
bowels, because a blessing is the daughter of tears,
and truth is the son of love."

Then I sat under the shade of the tree of my lonely soul
in that field away from the path of time.

Be still, my heart, until dawn.

Be still, for the air is charged with the odor of the dead,
and it cannot take on the sweetness of your breath.

Listen, my heart, and hear me speak.

Yesterday my thought was like a ship, rocked upon the
waves of the sea, and tossed by the winds from shore
to shore.

And the ship of my thought was empty save of seven
vessels filled to the brim with various hues and shades
like the rays of the rainbow.

And there came a time when I found myself weary of
     drifting upon the face of the waters, and I said,
"I will go back with the empty ship of my thought to
     the harbor of the town where I was born."
So, I began to paint the sides of my ship with colors,
     some yellow as the setting sun, some green as the
     heart of Spring, some blue as the heart of the sky,
     some red as melted crimson;
And I sketched upon the sails and rudder of my ship
     strange images which drew and delighted the eye and
     the mind.
And the ship of my thought revealed itself as the vision
     of a prophet floating between the two infinities, the
     sea and the sky.
And when I entered the harbor of my town the people
     came to meet me with jubilation and praise, and they
     led me to the city amidst trumpets and the sound of
     flutes.
This they did because the outside of my ship was
     beautified and alluring,
But not one among them asked, What had I brought in
     my ship from beyond the sea?
And not one perceived that I had returned with an
     empty ship to the harbor.

Then I said secretly, to myself, "Men have been deceived by the seven vessels full of colors which belied their vision and their minds."

A year after I embarked upon the ship of my thought and ploughed the seas again.

I sailed to the islands of the East and gathered there myrrh and frankincense and gold, and brought them to my ship.

And I sailed to the isles of the North and fetched ebony and ivory and rubies and emeralds and all precious stones.

I sailed to the South, and there I found and gathered silks and garments and porphyry.

And to the isles of the West I sailed, and carried away gleaming swords and haughty spears, and a wealth of weapons.

I filled the ship of my thought with the treasures and wonders of the earth, and came back to the harbor of my town and said,

"Now my countrymen will indeed glorify me, and rightly so. And they will lead me into the city amid songs and trumpetings, and justly."

But when I reached the shore none came out to meet
    me, and I entered the street of my city and none
    turned to look at me;
And I stood in the market-place telling the people what
    I had brought them of the fruits and the wonders of
    earth,
And they but glanced at me with mockery, and laughed
    and turned from me,
Sad I returned to the harbor wondering and grieved. But
    I had hardly sighted my ship when I saw that which
    I had neglected in the midst of my journeys and my
    desires:
The waves of the sea had washed away the paint from
    the sides of my ship, and revealed it as a skeleton,
And the storms and the winds and the heat of the
    sun had faded the images from the sails and they
    appeared like a tattered gray garment.
I had collected the precious and choice things of the
    world in a coffin which floated upon the face of the
    waters and came back to my people.
But my people cast me out because their eyes could see
    naught but external show.

And that very hour I left the ship of my thought and
    went to the city of the dead and sat among the
    whitened graves thinking of their secrets.

Be still, my heart, until dawn.
Be still, because the raging tempest mocks the
    whispering of your innermost being;
And the caves of the valley shall not echo the sounds of
    the strings of your harp.
Be still, my heart, for he who awaits dawn with patience,
    dawn will embrace him eagerly.
Here come dawn, my heart—speak then, if you have the
    power of words.
Here comes the procession of the day, my heart.
Has the stillness of night left in your depth a song to
    meet the dawn?
Here are flocks of doves and thrushes fluttering about
    the outskirts of the valley.
Has the awe of night left in your wings enough force
    that you may fly with them?
Behold, the shepherds leading their sheep from the
    folds.
Have the shadows of night left you the strength to
    follow them to the green pasture?

Behold, the young boys and the youths walk leisurely
toward the vineyards.
Will you not rise and follow them?
Rise, my heart, rise and walk with them.
Night is gone and the fears of night have vanished with
its dark dream.
Arise, my heart and raise your voice in song, for he who
does not share with dawn its song is surely the son of
darkness.

The Deeper Pain

(Undated)

To burn but not to shine, that is a great pain, but not to burn at all is the greater pain.

To have a full heart and an empty hand is pain indeed, but to have a full hand and find no one to receive it is a greater pain.

To be a cripple at the foot of the mountain of your heart's desire is a great pain, but to reach the top of the mountain and find yourself alone, that is the deeper pain.

To have a song in your spirit but not the voice to sing it is to know great pain, but to have both the song and the voice yet to find no one to listen is the greater pain.

Once I stood, a beggar, at the gate of the temple.

Night veiled all things, and my hand stretched forth was still empty.

At that hour, my friend, I knew pain.

But seven moons after that I stood in the portico of the temple to tell of spring in the forest,

And spring in the heart of a maiden,

And spring as the beginning of the race.

And no one listened to me. That was the greater pain.

The Sufist

(Undated)

Thanks unto the Lord,

We have no possessions,

Nor have we a possessor.

And we have no mate nor descendant nor kin.

We walk the earth a shadow

Seen only by those in whose eyes the shadow is hidden.

We laugh for the tragedy in the day;

And we weep for the laughter thereof.

And we are a spirit,

And you say, "How strange."

But we say, "How strange is your body."

Farewell.

THE EGOTIST

(October 11, 1929)

My memory is failing, but I still remember certain
  happenings of my yesterday.
I remember the hour in which the Tower of Babylon
  fell down. I was then on the bank of the Euphrates
  casting my net for fish, and about me the sparrows
  were chirping in the sun.
I remember when the two-horned Alexander died. I had
  a farm not far from his camp, and on that very night
  my cow gave birth to a godly calf.
And I remember this also: the last time I was being
  stoned to death—a girl was picking up a stone to
  hurl at me, and she found underneath the stone a
  golden coin. She picked it up and ran away crying,
  "Mother, mother mine, see what I have found."
And I remember when Troy fell. I fought as all Trojans
  fought. But upon that night when the Wooden Horse
  was dragged into the city, I was with my beloved in
  my mother's chamber and we had two lyres.
And my beloved sang as she had never sung before, nor
  after.

Part Three

Sayings and Aphorisms

The Burden

The difference between me and the other man is this: I see the image of my own face in the mirror, and he sees the image of his neighbor.

～✦～

I am busy with Today because I understand Today. For often I go to the house of Tomorrow and from her windows Today is clear like Yesterday.

Over yonder, below that grey mist, live men who are trying to explain yesterday. They are the philosophers. And men who are trying to col tomorrow. They are moralists. But here alone on these heights, I am busy with Today.

～✦～

A woman said to me "I shall not marry until I have made and made magnificent my unborn children."

～✦～

I always doubt what I desire to express when I find myself over-expressive.

～✦～

Is it not strange that you remember more often the man who disagreed with you, than the man who agreed with you?

～✦～

They would give me to drink of the milk of human kindness, and I am grateful. But would to heaven they might know that I have been weaned before I was born.

A spiritual man, a man of the spirt, is he who had experienced all that is physical, listened attentively to all the body-songs, then said to himself, "In very truth I cannot see the difference between the one song and the other songs. To mine eyes one valley is as deep as the other valley, and one mountain is as high as the other mountain.

———

Truth begotten by discussion is truth still-born.

———

Perchance allegiance is a form of insult to the ally. Perchance: its opposite is dignified respect.

———

Sweetness is much closer to bitterness than to the tainted.

———

Some praise is strangely similar to defame.

———

A coward taught me how to seem brave. Oh what I coward I have been.

———

Life kisses our faces gently every dawn and at every eventide. But life has a way of laughing at our deeds between dawn and eventide.

~

Even these that you call the laws of everyday life are obedient to the laws of everyday life.

How similar our saying "Yesterday," to our saying "Eternal past"; and how like our saying "Tomorrow," to our saying "Forever and forever, amen."

~

Behold, a strange case; Whatever there is in me of virtue has brought me naught but pain and that which is vicious in me has never harmed me. Yet I am still pulling with the rope of virtue I would see to what further trouble that white rope maiden would lead me.

~

The disease of a nation is in him who would now sow a seed, nor raise a stone upon a stone, nor would he weave the cloth, but who would deal in politics and in high-sounding oratory.

~

A stranger in a land may find comfort in another stranger in that land. But he who is a stranger in thought and spirit will find no comfort in any land.

The would-be philosopher is like unto a mirror that reflects but cannot see, and like a cave that echoes the sound of voices but cannot hear them.

My friend, do not ever forget that the most telling line in a poem is still dwelling either in the shyness or in the proud dignity of the poet's heart.

In my weaker moments I was taught originality by the multicolored parrots from South America.

There is naught that calls our love for the living so much as our regret for the dead.

I love children, but not with moustache and beard; and I love old men, but not in cradles.

How far am I from human beings when I am amongst them, and how near am I to them when I am far from them.

The freedom of him who is over-proud of his freedom is a form of slavery.

⌐✦⌐

In faith we can move all mountains. Now let us move the mountains in our souls and leave those of the earth to their serene majesty.

⌐✦⌐

Even if you make your back a bridge I will not cross.

⌐✦⌐

Charm is the art of saying "yes" without seeming over-attentive, and of saying "no" without frowning, and of making the other person say "yes" and "no" guilelessly.

⌐✦⌐

Many of our good intentions are like throwing pennies to birds. Some of our bad intentions are not so foolish.

⌐✦⌐

There is no such thing as a truth that hurts. That which hurts is but a stupid fact made impertinent.

⌐✦⌐

Man at his best is a desire, not an established order.

⌐✦⌐

If you would understand the other person you should be a mirror rather than a sponge.

⚬

People open their doors even before I knock at their doors. But that door which my spirit seeks remains unopened.

⚬

I had lost my way at dusk and I was weary. Then the western sky leaned over me and shook all her pink fingers in my face and said, "How could you doubt me, my child?"

⚬

A young man came to me and said, "Show me the way." And I answered, "My soul was wedded to the virtues, and we begat nothing. Then I left the virtues and gave myself to the fearlessness and desires, and we begat life."

⚬

A prophet once said to me, "Would that I might play hide and seek with little children. But how can I? What would my disciples think of me?"

⚬

In our thirst we come to the river of life and drink deep, and we are glad. But the sweet water itself is thirsty and it drinks us while we drink it.

⚬

Why do you give candles to the blind and deem your-
selves generous?

—⁘—

My friend, if it were not for bitter dawn of separations,
we would not find a lovely day among the days.

Indifference is a dead self. With these mine own hands
I buried it.

—⁘—

There are those who would give you all that they them-
selves have no need for, and they deem it generosity; and
there are those who spend themselves upon your day and
the life of your day, and they deem it a gift made unto
you. Oh, the pity of it all.

—⁘—

Speaking of kindly gifts, I want people to give me that
which They need more than I do.

—⁘—

There is a trick in giving which is greater than giving.

—⁘—

I know I shall move with the wind when I am dead, and
I know I shall move toward the west with a will. Please, I
beg you, do not be disturbed, for I shall not take any of
your possessions with me.

Now my brethren, let us have religion in life, and not out of this black book.

⚬

When tenderness is not the flower of strength, it is but fear seeing her own image in a mirror.

⚬

Your fear of what they call evil is but your doubt (lack of faith) in what you deem goodness.

⚬

If you would indeed be gracious you would invite again and yet again the man who insults your servants, and who would fall asleep, snoring, at your board.

⚬

In the tavern of life the curious seek the talented, the talented depend on the genius, and he rarely pays for the wine and why should he?

⚬

Wisdom without beauty is like a house without a roof.

⚬

Some men deem it an insult if you do not consider them enough to hate them.

The thieves I lived with taught me mathematics; I had to count my fingers after shaking hands.

⌒

(Editor's Note: this following saying is similar to that of one in "The Forerunner": "And I turned to the saint and said, 'Wherefore did you accuse yourself of uncommitted crimes? See you not this man went away no longer believing in you?' And the saint answered, 'It is true he no longer believes in me. But he went away much comforted.'")

How often have I accused myself of uncommitted crimes simply to make others feel comfortable in my presence.

⌒

A child playing with a skull, a red rose growing in the snow, a girl dancing upon the grave, a tiger sleeping in the temple—these things I always love to see.

⌒

None is so poor as he who is hungry for experiences. And none is so helpless as he who is willing to give but finds no one to take.

⌒

Necessity is the mother of little inventions. Great things are the children of ecstasy.

⌒

I know a woman who lived among the hills. She had a husband and she begat five daughters and four sons.

And when her husband died, and she buried him, and all her children died, the one after the other, and she buried them, all.

With her own hands she dug their graves among the hills, alone she buried them.

No one but myself knew she gave them birth, and no one knows now that she buried them among the hills.

⤙⤚

"Oh yes, I have loved a woman. She is dead now. And how often have I rubbed my eyes before her beauty to know whether I was asleep or awake."

Here we breed in these little houses. But do you not know that as a protest against slavery there are animals that refuse to breed in cages?

⤙⤚

When the soul of a city is weary of its body it steals to the wilderness whence it came, to die in peace. I have known cities with departed souls.

⤙⤚

Seven thousand years ago, at the foot of a mountain, I beheld a dog biting a dead lion. Then I lost my respect for the living and my fear of the dead.

Art is either a racial memory recalled, or a racial anticipation.

Millions died for Christ. He healed only a few.

How many dig their graves with their tongues?

Friendship is a ceaseless sense of giving joy.

Be perfectly negative and you will possess all the virtues man has conceived, but none of Mine.

Form is the fruit of a longing within.
Color is the reflection of an influence without.

Prophecy is but forecasting in the nature of the soul.

I will find one perfect friend ere I die.

Said a soldier to a physician, "You can erase the wounds from my face, but who shall erase the wounds from my heart?"

———

Those who will laugh at your gain, whatever it may be, are in truth laughing at their loss.

———

The only man who can tell you what to do or what not to do under any circumstance is the man married to your former wife. Heed him, and profit of his wisdom.

———

Weariness is a knowledge not yet digested.

———

Little success stiffens the neck of the little souls, and it softens the vitals of him who is still growing before the face of the sun.

But to the full-grown and the seasoned it is but a belly-ache that must needs have a potion to ease the pain.

———

Much do they speak of sex in these days. I do not know what is not sex. My neighbor is perplexed about it, and unhappy. He does not know how to gaze at the stars or at his own mirror.

A man reveals his secret to another man who hides the same secret. Afterward they both regret it.

Jealousy is a crippled memory of things unattained, but the pangs of jealousy may turn crutches to help the cripple towards attainment.

I do not know whether you shall be born again or not, but I say to you, take heed, my friend, take heed before you die.

Temptation has two voices: one says, "I am the command of your forefathers," and the other cries, "I am but the fulfillment of your own willingness."

A wall does not divide neighbor and neighbor. Distance is never distance between a heart and a heart.

Cult is never religion. Beat yourself to the sun, or to your own hell and get rid of it.

Seek beauty, create beauty, worship beauty. But if the power to seek is not given to you, nor the power to create, nor the power to worship, then go back to your father's farm, or come to me that I may give you a greater hunger for beauty.

Would you indeed, get rid of all wars? Then let women conduct the next war.

One day as I walked in my garden I thought my neighbors, old and young, gazed at me strangely, then whispered to each other, "The wanderer loves a woman. He loves the woman in the white tower across the valley."

All day long they looked at me from their windows in bewilderment and spoke of my love for a woman. And I was amazed for I knew not that I loved a woman. Yet there was upon me the desire of knowing.

And that very day at dusk, I left my garden and walked towards the white tower across the valley saying to myself, "How strange that my neighbors know of me that which I know not."

One of the other secrets of art is in expressing what the other person does not dare to express, or does not know how to express.

Women wink at the infinite and say, "Oh, let man work."

⌒‿⌒

Should you care to know the secret of a man do not try to learn what he has attained, but rather for what he is longing.

⌒‿⌒

He who gazes over-long at near miniatures may find it difficult to see the beauty of the vast distant pictures painted by our Lord.

⌒‿⌒

Ambition is a form of work.

⌒‿⌒

In very truth you cannot hear the songs of the fields until you have digested the noise of the city. But the noise of the city is good. It sharpens your ears.

⌒‿⌒

All happenings come to pass at an inevitable time. And there is a comfort in this simple godly principle.

⌒‿⌒

A praise finds me shy. But strange to say, a disfame leaves me an over-weening creature before the entire world.

Never have I known a poet without the desire in my heart to escape the worldlings.

Never have I thought of Jesus without seeing Him, a babe, looking into the face of his mother, Marianne, for the first time; or a giant, crucified, looking upon the face of His mother for the last time.

Spirits are flame and these bodies are but their ashes.

We are all fighters in the battle of life. Some of us lead and some of us are lead. But why turn the loveliness of life into a battle only God will make clear to us, not here, but beyond the horizon.

Part Four

Drafts of Passages from
The Earth Gods

The Greater Self

"The Ten Pities"

(Undated)

(Editor's Note: this poem appears in "The Garden of the Prophet" as "Pity the Nation." Gibran's draft title was "The Ten Pities" and a few of his writings did not appear in the final form.)

My friends and my road fellows

Pity the nation that is full of beliefs and empty of
religion.

Pity the nation that is a labyrinth of streets and has
forgotten its fields.

Pity the nation that wears a cloth it does not weave, eats
a bread it does not harvest and drinks a wine that
flows not from it's own wine press.

Pity the nation that claims the bully as hero, and that
deems the glittering conqueror bountiful.

Pity the nation that despises a passion in it's dreams, yet
submits in it's awakening.

Pity the nation that raises not it's voice save when it
walks in a funeral, brags not except among it's ruins
and will rebel not until it's neck is laid between the
sword and the block.

Pity the nation whose statesman is a fox, whose
philosopher is a juggler and whose art is the art of
patching and mimicking.

Pity the nation that welcomes each new ruler with
   trumpetings, and farewells him with hootings, only to
   welcome another ruler with trumpeting again.
Pity the nation whose sages are dumb with years, and
   whose strong men are yet in the cradle.
Pity the nation divided into and each fragment deeming
   itself a nation.

Untitled Poem

(Undated, translated from his own Arabic)

(Editor's Note: the following was found as written in the University of North Carolina collection. These lines appear seemingly as one poem. They are all used in "The Earth Gods" among the sayings by The First God and are dispersed throughout the work.)

And the laughing sea mocks your abiding stability
And what hope is there for you and me?

What shifting of worlds,
What new purpose in the heavens
Shall claim you?
Does the womb of the virgin infinite
Bear the seed of your redeemed,
One mightier than your vision,
Whose hand shall deliver you from captivity?

Oh my soul, my soul,
Sad is your sweetness, and silent is your face;
And in your eye-sockets the shadows of night
sleep peacefully.
Yet dangerous is your calm,
And you are terrible.

THE YOUNG GOD

(Undated, found without attribution to The Earth Gods)

(Editor's Note: the following was found as written in the University of North Carolina collection and is a draft of a segment of "The Earth Gods." Originally spoken by "The Young God," these lines are attributed to The Third God. The parenthetical comments do not appear in "The Earth Gods.")

Brothers, my solemn brothers,
The girls has found the singer
And beheld his raptured face.
Panther-like she guides her subtle steps
Through rustling vines and [ferns],
And with parted lips and eyes arrested
She gazes upon his youth as one in dream.

Brothers, my heedless brothers,
What other god in passion has woven this web of
scarlet and white?
What unbridled star has gone astray?
What secret keeps night from day,
And whose hand is upon our world?

(The earth breathes
And we live.
The earth calls back its breath
And we die.)

Aloneness

About the Author

KAHLIL GIBRAN (1883–1931) was a writer, poet, and Lebanese nationalist and visual artist. His teaching fable, *The Prophet*, remains one of the bestselling inspirational works of all time.

About the Editor

DALTON EINHORN is the son of Virginia Hilu, the editor who produced the first-ever book from the Gibran/Haskell archives at the University of North Carolina. In following her footsteps after her tragic young death, he gained permissions to return to the collection, in which he discovered over 150 Gibran pieces never before published.